The
HEALING
POWER
of Jesus

Robert Abel

Valentine Publishing House
Denver, Colorado

Valentine Publishing House LLC
P.O. Box 27422
Denver, Colorado 80227

The Scripture quotations contained herein are from the *New Revised Standard Version Bible,* copyright 1989 by the Division of Christian Education of the National Council of the Churches of Christ in the U.S.A., and are used by permission. All rights reserved.

Scripture texts used in this work are taken from the *New American Bible* with Revised New Testament, © 1986 Confraternity of Christian Doctrine. All rights reserved. No part of the *New American Bible* may be reproduced in any form without permission in writing from the copyright owner. Permission to reprint the text does not indicate endorsement.

Cover Graphics—Desert Isle Design LLC

Library of Congress Control Number: 2006922580

Publisher's Cataloging-in-Publication Data

Abel, Robert.
    The Healing Power of Jesus / Robert Abel / 2nd Edition.

        p. : ill. ; cm.

        ISBN–10: 0-9711536-6-3
        ISBN–13: 978-0-9711536-6-0
        Includes bibliographical references.

1. Spiritual healing. 2. Healing—Religious aspects—Christianity. 3. Faith—Biblical teaching. 4. Spiritual Warfare. I. Title.

BT732.5 .A24 2006
234/.131

                                        2006922580

Printed in the United States of America.

Table of Contents

*Great crowds came to him, having with them
the lame, the blind, the deformed, the mute,
and many others. They placed them at his feet,
and he cured them. The crowds were amazed
when they saw the mute speaking, the deformed
made whole, the lame walking, and the blind
able to see, and they glorified the God of Israel.*

Matthew 15:30–31

Introduction

In the beginning, God created the heavens and the earth. The Spirit of the Lord spoke unto the dust of the ground and said, *"Let us make humankind in our image, according to our likeness."*[1] Instantly a perfect man arose. His name was Adam, and he was created in complete unity, beauty and harmony with his Creator.

Then God said, *"It is not good that the man should be alone; I will make him a helper as his partner."*[2] So the Lord caused a deep sleep to fall upon the man. He took one of his ribs and closed up its place with flesh. The rib that the Lord took from the man, he made into a woman.

Adam was not crippled from birth. Eve did not have muscular dystrophy. She did not suffer from fibromyalgia or asthma. Adam was not stricken with cancer or leukemia. They were created in the image and likeness of God in perfect health, beauty and strength.

When Adam and Eve rebelled against God and committed the first sin, evil entered the world and separated mankind from God's blessings and protection.

God, being pure spirit, love, light and truth, could no longer relate to his beloved children in the same way. Once Adam and Eve were separated from God's protection, evil started attacking them with every kind of spiritual and physical sickness.

God in his loving kindness devised a plan and immediately started working with all future generations. He tried to convince Cain to offer an acceptable sacrifice and warned him about the ever-present danger by saying, *"Sin is lurking at the door; its desire is for you, but you must master it."*[3] Unfortunately, the presence of darkness that was lurking at Cain's door overpowered him, and he killed his brother Abel.

After Cain committed the sin of murder, the *ancient serpent, who is called the Devil and Satan, the deceiver of the whole world,*[4] acquired an even stronger influence over humanity. Along with this wicked and deadly influence, sin, sickness and diseases covered the entire land. It got so bad that at one point God was sorry he created humankind and decided to remove them from the face of the earth.

After starting over with Noah, God began working with Abraham, Isaac and Jacob to create a royal priesthood, a chosen people to be his own. He allowed the Israelites to suffer over 430 years in captivity in the land of Egypt. He worked many powerful miracles through Moses to set them free. After parting the Red Sea, God spoke an agreement to them saying, *"If you will listen carefully to the voice of the Lord your God, and do what is right in his sight, and give heed to his commandments and keep all his statutes, I will not bring upon*

*you any of the diseases that I brought upon the Egyptians;
for I am the Lord who heals you."[5]*

All the Israelites had to do was fulfill their end of
the agreement, and they would have God's blessings
and protection.

1. They had to listen carefully to the voice of the Lord
   their God. (Are you practicing contemplative
   prayer?)
2. They had to do what is right in his sight. (Are you
   practicing obedience?)
3. They had to give heed to his commandments and
   keep his statutes. (Are you practicing holiness?)

If God's children continued to walk in obedience
and holiness, then God would not allow evil forces to
inflict their bodies with all the diseases found in the
land of Egypt.

Unfortunately, the Israelites continued to sin, so
God set up a temporary system of repentance. The
system worked great for a time, but soon after, the
Israelites' hearts grew hardened. They were constantly
committing sins and constantly performing purification
rituals in the temple.

Because God desired more holiness from his children, he sent the prophet Ezekiel to declare the coming of a new covenant: *I will sprinkle clean water upon
you, and you shall be clean from all your uncleannesses,
and from all your idols I will cleanse you.*

*A new heart I will give you, and a new spirit I will put
within you; and I will remove from your body the heart of*

stone and give you a heart of flesh. I will put my spirit within you, and make you follow my statutes and be careful to observe my ordinances. Then you shall live in the land that I gave to your ancestors; and you shall be my people, and I will be your God.[6]

In the Old Covenant, the penalty for sin was sickness, death and disease. In the New Covenant the penalty remains the same, except instead of placing our sins on an innocent sheep and allowing that animal to pay the death penalty on our behalf, we can now place our sins on the innocent Lamb of God.

In the fullness of time, God sent his only begotten Son into the world to pay the death penalty for our sins. God's only begotten Son became man. He lived a sinless life and offered his body to be tortured and crucified. He willingly took upon himself the sins and sickness of the world, so that everyone who repents can be forgiven.

By accepting the Lord's sacrifice on the cross and following his teachings, you can now be restored into perfect fellowship with the Father. Once you are completely restored into God's fellowship, not only will the Lord's healing power flow into your life, but it will also flow through you, into the lives of others.

The same miracle-working power that was available in the life of Christ is available for you right now. All you need to do is surrender your life and healing process into the Lord's hands.

What are you waiting for? Jesus is the great Physician. Jesus touched everyone who asked him for healing. He desires that you walk in perfect health and holiness with him now and forever.

The time is now—the kingdom of heaven is at hand!

1

The Power of Desire

When Donna was younger she was moving a heavy appliance from a high shelf and tore a membrane in her abdominal wall. Every now and then, she would complain about the pain, so one day I said to her, "Would you like to pray for healing?"

"Yeah, right," she said.

"What's better, a doctor sewing plastic mesh inside your body, or the Lord, Jesus?"

"I gotta do something soon, it's really starting to hurt me," Donna said as she put her hand on her stomach.

"The Lord never turned anyone away for healing. He took all the sins and sickness of the world into his own body, so that you could be made whole."

"I'm ready to pray whenever you are," she said.

"The healing power of Jesus is already here. All you need to do is tap into it. Just close your eyes and picture Jesus coming to lay hands on you."

Donna closed her eyes and after a few minutes, she looked more relaxed. I asked her to place her hands on the area that needed healing, and we commanded the tear in her abdominal wall to be sealed in the name, power and authority of Jesus.

"Now, all you need to do is receive your healing through the power of faith. It doesn't matter how it feels. Healing power has already entered your body, just accept it and spend a lot of time in praise and thanksgiving."

The very next day, I was delivering a computer to Donna's house, and I wanted to help her set it up before leaving. When it came time to lift the monitor out of the box, I asked Donna to give me a hand.

"I can't pick that up—I have a hernia," she said.

A shocking moment of silence fell over both of us. "Wait a minute," I said. "We just prayed for your healing yesterday. Do you have a hernia, or has the Lord healed you? Have you accepted the Lord's healing power, or do you want to use it as an excuse?"

Deep within Donna's heart she was holding on to her disability. Over the years she had used the hernia as an excuse to get out of doing work. The computer monitor didn't weigh more than 15 pounds. She didn't even try to lift it. She automatically gave the same excuse that she had used most of her life.

Jesus knows our needs before we ask. Jesus' healing power was available for Donna to invite into her body at any time, except Jesus doesn't violate anyone's free will. So long as Donna had a subconscious need, reason or a desire to hold on to her infirmity, the Lord's healing power would be hindered from flowing into her body.

Donna had a choice to make. Did she want to fully surrender herself into the Lord's healing hands, or did she want to hold on to the benefits that she was receiving through her sickness?

After I told her about the power of faith, we had a long talk about her desire to be healed. After that, she stopped complaining about the pain. She never used the hernia as an excuse again, and to this day, she has made a complete recovery.

Another story about the desire to be healed comes from a man living on the streets of Jerusalem. Late one afternoon, when Jesus was walking through the market area, he came to the pool called Bethesda. There were five magnificent porticoes built from stone blocks with elaborate cornerstones set in the center of each archway.

In the center of the cobblestone courtyard was a large spring-fed pool. Surrounding the pool were many invalids, including the lame, blind and the paralyzed. Many of them had spent their whole lives living in the area, begging alms.

Some would lie near the water's edge, waiting for a supernatural force to stir up the pool. Legend had it that every so often an angel would descend from heaven and touch the tip of his wing on the water, creating a small rippling effect. The first person who plunged into the pool after the angel appeared would be miraculously healed.

As Jesus entered the courtyard, he recognized a

man who had been there 38 years. The man had given up all hope of being the first one into the water. He couldn't walk, and was lying in a shady area near the stone partition. His skin was dark brown and weathered from being out in the elements for most of his life. As Jesus approached him, the man looked up as if startled by his presence. Jesus looked through the discouragement into his eyes and said, *"Do you want to be made well?"*[1]

At first the question seemed very distasteful. The man had been lying around for 38 years trying to receive healing power from a magic pool, and Jesus had the audacity to ask, "Do you want to be made well?"

As soon as Jesus asked the question, the Holy Spirit began to work in the man's heart. If the man received his healing from the Lord, he would no longer have an excuse to lie around the pool all day. His entire way of life would have to change. If he wasn't allowed to beg anymore, he may be forced into the fields to work the harvest.

Maybe the man liked receiving attention from the townspeople who visited the pool. Maybe he liked sympathy and wanted people to feel sorry for him. Maybe he was trying to prove how holy he was for suffering like a self-righteous martyr for 38 years.

As the Holy Spirit took the man deeper into his heart, he realized that even his religious beliefs were being challenged. If Jesus had the power to heal him, then maybe Jesus really was the Messiah that everyone had been taking about. If he accepted Jesus' healing power, would he also have to accept Jesus' Lordship over his life?

As the love and compassion of Jesus' presence continued to pierce the man's heart, the truth was finally disclosed. He wanted healing at any cost, but he didn't know how to receive it, so he said, *"Sir, I have no one to put me into the pool when the water is stirred up; and while I am making my way, someone else steps down ahead of me."²*

Jesus said to him, *"Stand up, take your mat and walk."³*

At once the man was made well. As soon as the crippled man accepted the Lord's healing power, he was made well. He stood up, picked up his mat and began walking around, praising God.

If you are sick, Jesus wants to ask you the same question—do you want to be made well? You cannot hold on to your sickness and at the same time expect the Lord to heal you. You cannot make agreements with your sickness and suffering and at the same time expect Jesus to take them away. Jesus never violates anyone's free will.

If the lame man believed he was doing God a favor by lying around and suffering, then his religious beliefs would have prevented the flow of Jesus' healing power. Before the man could be healed, Jesus had to ask him a very important question. Do you want to be made well, or do you want to lie around and suffer?

If you are sick, how bad do you want to be made well? Are you willing to accept Jesus as your Lord,

Master and Savior? Are you willing to change your religious beliefs about healing? Are you willing to change your theological beliefs about suffering? Are you willing to have Jesus turn your entire life upside down?

If so, you may want to spend some time in prayer right now and invite the Lord Jesus into your heart. Ask the Holy Spirit to show you the source of your infirmity. Go boldly before the throne of grace and keep pursuing God until you get an answer. Go with all the passion that is required, and hold fast to every spiritual principle advised by the apostle James:

If any of you is lacking in wisdom, ask God, who gives to all generously and ungrudgingly, and it will be given you. But ask in faith, never doubting, for the one who doubts is like a wave of the sea, driven and tossed by the wind; for the doubter, being double-minded and unstable in every way, must not expect to receive anything from the Lord.[4]

Start pursuing God with all your strength. Do not give up until you receive an answer from the Lord. Ask God to shine the light of his Holy Spirit deep into your heart and show you everything that keeps you attached to your infirmity. Ask God to show you the source where it came from, and how it has access to your life. After you receive answers to these questions, ask the Lord to show you the next step in your healing process.

The Power of Truth

One day a contractor hired me to make structural repairs in a basement that he was finishing. After agreeing to meet his superintendent on the job site, we were greeted by a large, unfriendly dog that started growling at us.

"Don't worry about old Rex," the superintendent said. "He will just sit there and do that all day."

After the superintendent showed me the steel I-beam that needed to be replaced, he left me alone with my helpers to finish the job. I didn't think any more about the dog until I went upstairs and I noticed the garage door had been left open.

"Where's the dog?" I said.

"I don't know. He went outside," one of my helpers said.

"If the homeowner's dog gets away, don't you think we're responsible? Now, go down the street and look for him," I said.

After walking around a little, I returned to find the dog in the front yard. I grabbed his collar and started taking him back into the garage. All of a sudden the dog halted, turned his head and bit my arm.

Immediately, I put both hands on his collar and wrestled him to the ground.

"Hurry up and get over here! Get ahold of the dog's back legs. We need to carry him through the house and put him in the backyard."

Mike ran over as fast as he could and grabbed the dog's hind legs. Bill ran ahead of us to open the doors. While we were carrying the dog through the house, somehow he got ahold of my left index finger. I couldn't get my hand out of his mouth. The dog's rear molars ripped through my leather glove, straight into my flesh and down to the bone.

After we were able to secure the dog in the backyard, I went to the kitchen sink and started cleaning the wound. I had to pull dog hair and loose pieces of flesh out of the wound. I looked in every bathroom in the house for some medical supplies, but there were none.

I couldn't even find a Band-Aid. All I could find was a tiny bottle of vodka in the kitchen cabinet, so I used it to clean the wound. Afterward, I wrapped my finger with electrical tape and went back to work.

As I continued making repairs to the I-beam, my hand started hurting more and more. By the end of the day, my hand had swollen so much that I could no longer bend my finger.

After finishing the job that evening, I went to the doctor and told him what happened. He said, "We take dog bites very seriously. There's all kinds of bacteria in a dog's mouth." As the doctor immersed my hand in a container of disinfectant, he said, "If your arm gets red streaks, or if the swelling increases, we are going to admit you to the hospital for IV treatment."

I could feel flashes of fear coming over me. My face started blushing as he explained all the dangers that were involved with a dog bite wound. After giving me a five-minute lecture, he left me in the room to allow my finger more time to soak. As soon as he did, I started praying to bind up the spirit of fear and all the negative words that were spoken against me.

The next day when I called the superintendent to explain the situation, he said, "You had better take all your penicillin. Dog bite wounds are very serious. You could lose your hand."

"The pharmacy ran out," I said. "They could only fill half the order. Can you guys cover the other half of the expense?"

"How much money is your hand worth if they have to cut it off? If you don't take all your penicillin, the infection will spread through your entire body."

After getting off the phone, I took authority over all the negative word curses the superintendent had spoken against me. My hand was recovering nicely, but deep in my heart, I was hurt. I was angry at the dog for attacking me. I was upset with my helpers for leaving the door open. I was fearful about all the negative warnings the doctor had spoken, and I didn't want to spend any more money on penicillin.

After a few weeks passed, I called the homeowner's

insurance company to see if they would reimburse me for the expense. After I explained the situation to the adjuster, he said, "There's only $5,000 in coverage."

After the insurance company paid the medical expenses, we settled on $1,000 for compensation. The insurance adjuster sent me a release of liability that needed to be signed by a witness, so I sent it to my attorney for review.

A few days later the adjuster called and asked if I had sent the paperwork back to his office. "Didn't my attorney call you?" I said.

"What attorney? Did you sign any papers with him?"

"My finger still hurts, and I think it's nerve damage. When I lift weights there's a funny sensation in my hand that wasn't there before. Like when I crumple up a piece of paper, it feels weird."

"Why don't you go back to your doctor and ask for a disability report? Then we can renegotiate your settlement."

My doctor said my hand was recovering nicely, but because I pressed him for a disability report, he suggested I see a disability specialist. After checking the phone book, I set another appointment hoping to find a doctor who would write a report telling the insurance company that my hand had suffered permanent damage.

The second doctor noted minor nerve damage, and after he ordered an X-ray, he suggested that I see a hand specialist. After visiting several more doctors, I was able to settle with the insurance company for more money.

The only problem was that after I had settled, my hand started getting worse. The minor nerve damage in my left index finger had evolved into a constant pain in all my knuckles. It felt like a form of arthritis. It seemed like bacteria from the dog's mouth, or chemical side effects from the penicillin, were causing arthritis in my joints.

Up to this point, I never took my injury very seriously. I had suffered hundreds of cuts and scrapes, and they always healed just fine, but for some reason, this was different. The arthritic condition had my full attention. After getting serious in prayer, I asked the Holy Spirit to shine his light deep into my heart to reveal the source of the problem.

After a lot of prayer, I came to the realization that my injury was both a medical and a spiritual problem. My situation was similar to a problem a crippled woman was experiencing the day she entered the synagogue when Jesus was teaching: *There appeared a woman with a spirit that had crippled her for eighteen years. She was bent over and was quite unable to stand up straight.*[1]

When Jesus saw her, he called her over and said, "Woman, you are set free from your ailment." When he laid his hands on her, immediately she stood up straight and began praising God.[2]

Afterward the leaders of the synagogue grew indignant because Jesus was healing on the Sabbath. The Lord responded to their objections by saying, *"Ought not this woman, a daughter of Abraham whom Satan bound for eighteen long years, be set free from this bondage on the sabbath day?"³*

The source of her medical condition was a demonic spirit. Satan had bound her for 18 long years. A spirit of infirmity was attacking her body. Somehow an evil spirit had acquired the right to enter into her body and cause a medical problem. After Jesus cast out the demonic spirit, the Holy Spirit entered her body, and she began to recover.

In the same way, the source of my medical condition was also coming from a spiritual and physical origin. When the dog was tearing into my finger, I was not filled with the peace, presence and joy of the Holy Spirit. I was under great stress, acting impatiently, trying to get the job ready before the welder arrived. I was angry with my helpers for letting the dog escape. I was still hurt because the dog annihilated my finger, and to make matters worse, I had cleaned my open wound with the homeowner's vodka.

After the Holy Spirit showed me all this, plus all the word curses from the doctors, I decided to see a priest to tell him what had happened. After the priest listened to my story, I asked him to pray for the healing of my hand, but nothing seemed to happen.

Because my condition was growing worse, I decided to use a meditative style of prayer to invite the Lord's healing power into the past event. I began the exercise by picturing Jesus and myself going back to the day when the angry construction worker was wrestling with the defensive dog.

When the divine presence of God entered my meditative scene, the angry construction worker realized the fullness of his wrongdoing. He let the dog go and turned around on his knees. Looking up into the Lord's loving eyes, he said, "Please forgive me. All of this is so very wrong. I'm sorry."

After the construction worker asked for forgiveness, Jesus healed the dog. As soon as I let him go, Rex started licking me in the face. In the meditative scene, Jesus filled the dog with love, and it overflowed into my heart. It was a beautiful and tearful time of healing with the Lord, and several days later, my hand felt much better. Every time I went back to the meditative scene with Jesus, the dog was still licking me in the face.

Even though my hand felt much better, it was not completely restored until the day the Lord spoke to me through Sacred Scripture. I was reading a verse that said, *the truth will make you free.*[4] As my thoughts were being transformed to God's thoughts, the Holy Spirit showed me the remaining hindrance that was preventing God's healing power from flowing into my hand.

The tiny amount of arthritic condition was allowed to remain because I was not operating in God's truth. I had created a lie, and through that lie, the sickness had a right to remain in my body. Deep in my heart, I wanted the insurance money more than I wanted the Lord's healing power.

If I truly wanted healing, I would have accepted Jesus' healing. I would have put my faith into action and expected my hand to recover. Instead, I went to several doctors, asking them to write disability reports, trying to prove that my hand was still sick and permanently disabled.

I was guilty of negative faith. Positive faith would have allowed God's healing power to flow into my life. Negative faith allowed the arthritic condition to remain. Did I want sickness and money, or did I want God and healing?

It is not possible to want my hand to be sick, and at the same time want my hand to be healed. By agreeing with the doctor's disability report and failing to bring my deception into the light of God's truth, I was allowing the spirit of infirmity to remain in my body. After I repented of my sins and made amends for my inappropriate actions, God's truth set me free.

If you are suffering a serious illness, the Holy Spirit wants to show you his version of the truth. Everybody has his or her own version of the truth. It was very easy for me to believe that I was an innocent victim of a vicious dog attack. I was even able to get many doctors to support my side of the story, but in God's eyes, I had entered an agreement with deception. My anger and sin of greed, along with the lack of openness to God's healing power, had opened the door for an evil spirit of infirmity to attack my body.

If you are sick, ask the Holy Spirit to shine the light of truth into your heart. Dig deep down into your past and examine every detail of your injury. How was your relationship with God before, during and after the time the illness first entered your life? Did you accept any curses or negative forms of faith from others? If so, ask the Holy Spirit to start replacing all the lies with the truth.

Take some time right now and get very serious in prayer before the Lord. You should be prepared to face a lot of internal resistance. If you have allowed lies from the enemy to enter your belief system, denounce all your self-willed and self-righteous ways, and humbly ask Jesus to set you free.

God desperately desires to set you free. God's truth has the power to set you free. Seek the truth with all your strength, and the truth will set you free.

3

The Power of Belief

It was a bright and sunny day when Jesus stepped out of the boat. The entire town had been anticipating his arrival. Before Peter could get the boat tied to the dock, a large crowd from all walks of life had gathered.

One woman knew deep in her heart that if she could just touch the hem of Jesus' garment that she would be healed. She was standing on the seashore watching the vast crowd as they approached from the distance. The soft sea breeze blew through her hair as anticipation welled up in her heart.

As Jesus moved closer, the power of the Holy Spirit came upon her. Many events from her past started flashing before her eyes. *She had endured much under many physicians, and had spent all that she had; and she was no better, but rather grew worse.*[1]

Every time she visited a doctor she experienced the same treatment. The physicians would label her with an incurable disease. Many of the doctors gave the disease different names, but all the names sounded menacing and life threatening. The more she believed in the sickness, the more power it acquired over her life.

As Jesus grew closer, the great crowd began to surround the woman. She held her position as the people pressed around her on all sides. Suddenly an opening appeared, her opportunity had arrived. She reached forward, and for a brief second, touched his cloak. *For she said, "If I but touch his clothes, I will be made well."*[2]

Immediately, her hemorrhage stopped, and she felt in her body that she was healed of her disease. All of a sudden, Jesus stopped and turned around. He was fully aware that healing power had gone into the woman, but for the sake of the crowd, and so that the woman could give proper praise to God, Jesus said, *"Who touched my clothes?"*[3]

His disciples could see that hundreds of people had been touching him, so they said, *"You see the crowd pressing in on you; how can you say, 'Who touched me?'"*[4]

Jesus began looking around, and *the woman, knowing what had happened to her, came in fear and trembling, fell down before him, and told him the whole truth.*[5] Jesus lifted her from the ground, looked into her eyes and said, *"Daughter, your faith has made you well; go in peace, and be healed of your disease."*[6]

The woman was healed through the power of her faith. There were many sick people in the crowd that day, and many were touching the Lord, but the one who received healing, received it through the power of her own faith. Instead of believing in her incurable disease, she made a choice to believe in Jesus. As soon as she put her faith into action, the healing power of Jesus was released, and she was made whole.

Faith is the spiritual pipeline that taps into the Lord's healing power. The Book of Hebrews says that *without faith it is impossible to please God.[7]* Faith is more than a mental belief that Jesus has the power to heal people. Faith is the actual instrument that allows God's healing power to flow into your life.

In almost all of the healings that Jesus performed, he accredited the release of his miracle-working power to the faith of the recipient. For example, two blind men started crying out to Jesus saying, *"Have mercy on us, Son of David!"[8]*

Jesus asked them, *"Do you believe that I am able to do this?"[9]*

They said to him, "Yes, Lord."[10]

After Jesus touched their eyes, he said, *"According to your faith let it be done to you." And their eyes were opened.[11]*

If the two men had maintained a stronger belief in their blindness, then their negative faith would have prevented the Lord's healing power from flowing into their eyes. As soon as the men opened their eyes and strained with all their might to see, the Lord's healing power flowed through their optical nerves, and they were healed.

Another case of an incurable disease being healed through the power of faith happened in the region of Tyre and Sidon. A Canaanite woman's daughter was very sick. No one could help her because a demonic spirit was attacking her little girl's body. So the woman approached Jesus and said, *"Have mercy on me, Lord, Son of David; my daughter is tormented by a demon."[12]*

At first Jesus objected to her request by saying, *"I*

was sent only to the lost sheep of the house of Israel."[13] But after the woman pleaded with him, Jesus granted her request by saying, *"Woman, great is your faith! Let it be done for you as you wish."*[14]

Before the little girl could be healed, her mother had to believe that Jesus had more power over the demonic influence than the evil spirit had over the little girl's body. If the Canaanite woman had a small amount of faith, a small amount of healing power would have been released. But because she had a great amount of faith, *her daughter was healed instantly.*[15]

Another example of an incurable illness caused by demonic spirits comes from the Book of Job. Satan had to go before God's throne to acquire permission before attacking this righteous man. Without God's permission, or without Job making agreements with evil through his sinful behaviors, Satan could not touch him, because Job was *blameless and upright, one who feared God and turned away from evil.*[16]

The Lord was so confident in Job's faithfulness, he said to Satan, *"Have you considered my servant Job? There is no one like him on the earth, a blameless and upright man who fears God and turns away from evil."*[17]

"Does Job fear God for nothing?" Satan said. *"Have you not put a fence around him and his house and all that he has, on every side? You have blessed the work of his hands, and his possessions have increased in the land. But stretch out your hand now, and touch all that he has, and he will curse you to your face."*[18]

The Lord said to Satan, *"Very well, all that he has is*

in your power; only do not stretch out your hand against him!"[19]

Satan immediately started attacking Job. He assigned many legions of fallen angels to destroy his finances and livelihood. These demonic forces attacked Job's servants, herds and flocks. They even had the power to stir up a deadly windstorm that caused a building to collapse on Job's family members.

After Satan had completely destroyed Job's life, finances and livelihood, he appeared before God's throne a second time, and the Lord said to him, *"Have you considered my servant Job? There is no one like him on the earth, a blameless and upright man who fears God and turns away from evil. He still persists in his integrity, although you incited me against him, to destroy him for no reason."*[20]

"Skin for skin! All that people have they will give to save their lives. But stretch out your hand now and touch his bone and his flesh, and he will curse you to your face."[21]

The Lord said to Satan, *"Very well, he is in your power; only spare his life."*[22]

So Satan went out from the presence of the Lord, and inflicted loathsome sores on Job, from the sole of his foot to the crown of his head.[23]

These sores were a medical condition being caused by a demonic source. Invisible spirits of infirmity were attacking Job's body causing cancerous sores to appear. Evil spirits were allowed to enter Job's flesh and cause what many doctors would diagnose as an incurable disease. Without the healing power of God, the demonic illness would have continued to spread throughout Job's body, and there would be nothing any medical treatment could do to help him recover.

Another example of demonic illness comes from the Gospel of Luke when Jesus met a man who could not speak. In order for the man to be healed, Jesus had to cast *out a demon that was mute; when the demon had gone out, the one who had been mute spoke.*[24] In this situation, a demonic spirit was causing the man's speech impediment. When the spirit that was attacking his vocal cords was commanded to leave, the man recovered.

Another example of demonic illness comes from the Gospel of Matthew where a man brought his son to Jesus for healing. The boy had been diagnosed with epilepsy, a chronic nervous disorder of the brain affecting consciousness and muscular control. The disciples tried to cast out the demon, but they could not, so Jesus said, *"Bring him here to me." And Jesus rebuked the demon, and it came out of him, and the boy was cured instantly.*[25]

In all these cases, the patient could have been very easily diagnosed with a medical condition, but in all these cases the source of the problem was a spiritual attack. Invisible and very subtle evil spirits had entered these people's lives and were causing serious medical problems.

If you are sick, you have a choice to make—are you going to put your faith in your doctor's diagnosis, or are you going to put your faith in the divine Physician?

Are you going to believe in an incurable disease, or are you going to believe that Jesus has the healing power of deliverance, and a burning desire to set you free?

If the source of your illness is coming from a spiritual condition, you may not be able to fully recover, unless you deal with the root cause. If an evil spirit has been attacking your body with a rare or incurable disease, like cancer, you may first need to believe in the devil's existence, before you will be able to drive it out of your body.

If your belief in the doctor's diagnosis is stronger than your belief in Jesus' healing power, break that bondage right now by the power of Jesus. Say the words out loud: I denounce you (spirit of cancer) in the name of Jesus. If a doctor cursed you with a certain number of days to live, break that curse right now in the name of Jesus. Say the words out loud: I break your hold over my life in the name of Jesus.

After you have finished breaking all the word curses spoken over your life, take several hours in prayer right away and ask Jesus to show you the source of your infirmity. Ask the Holy Spirit to shine his light of truth deep into your heart. Pray that all the lies and devices of the devil be destroyed.

Invite the miracle-working power of Jesus into your body, so that by believing in his divine healing power, you may be made whole.

4

The Power of Faith

Many years ago, a silver sports car pulled out in front of me. The driver was trying to make a left turn and realized there wasn't enough time. He came to a complete stop, blocking my lane of traffic. By the time I hit the brakes, hundreds of feet had already passed.

As I watched my car approach his with deadly force, my perception of time came to a complete standstill. I could hear the sound of tires screeching against the pavement. A thick cloud of gray smoke streamed out from underneath my front fenders. I could even see the look of terror on the other driver's face. It felt as though I was watching everything in slow motion.

Within seconds of impact, I forced the steering wheel hard to the left, but it was too late. My car clipped against his with just enough force to send me into a tailspin. After a jolting blow, I watched everything flip upside down, as my car spun airborne across the median.

Metal tearing against metal, the impact was devastating. I crashed head-on into a bright yellow school bus, traveling around 45 miles per hour. The front of the bus folded in like a crushed pop can. The force

ripped the engine and transmission out of my car and sent them flying toward a field 100 yards away.

I tried to hold on, but wasn't wearing a seat belt. The impact was too great. Just as my fragile body was about to be shredded over the sharp, jagged edges of metal and glass, God appeared!

Afterward, I found myself lying on the pavement next to my front tire. Looking up, I could see a large hole where I had escaped. God had miraculously ripped an opening through the side of my car, and saved my life from total destruction.

The accident blocked all four lanes of traffic, and soon many people began to gather. They formed a circle around me and watched as I lay on the ground praying. No one approached me until the paramedics arrived. I don't know why someone didn't try to comfort me, but it was the most painful part of the accident.

The next few days were extremely miserable. I had torn ligaments in both knees, my right thumb was broken, and I couldn't move my left arm because of a compound fracture to my collarbone. I felt completely helpless because I couldn't even get out of the hospital bed by myself.

After the doctors reattached my broken thumb with screws and pins, another doctor came into my room to look at my knees. I couldn't move my legs because of the pain. Both my knees were swollen to the size of softballs, and my legs were covered with huge gashes where the sharp, jagged edges of sheet metal from the car had cut through my flesh.

The doctor wanted to see how badly my tendons were damaged by performing a test. He wanted to put pressure on both knee joints to see how many ligaments were still holding my legs together. After he twisted the joint he said, "I felt about three-fourths of an inch. I would estimate between 70 to 90 percent of your ligaments and tendons have been torn away."

"What does that mean?" I asked.

"We will need to schedule surgery right away."

"How do you repair tendons?"

"We won't know until we get in there. We usually drill a series of holes through your bones and then weave the remaining ligaments through those holes to see if they will reattach."

"Can the ligaments reattach themselves?"

"No, they usually just float around inside your joint and deteriorate."

"I'm worried about the hospital bills. I don't have insurance. I'm afraid the bus driver and the school district are going to sue me."

After the doctor left the room, the old man in the bed next to me said, "Don't ya ever let them cut ya open like that!"

"Why, don't you trust the doctors?" I said.

"Ya see, I had a buddy that got that same kind of operation years ago. His legs got all infected. Them doctors crippled him. He's never been right since."

I didn't know what to do. I was desperate, broken

and hurting. All the doctors and nurses were extremely nice to me. It was very easy to trust them, because I was so vulnerable. I was lying there without much hope, in a state of total dependence. The old man had a good point, but then again, it was very easy to believe everything the doctors and nurses were telling me.

A few days later, I asked to go home. I was in tremendous pain, but I couldn't stand the thought of paying thousands of dollars for another night's stay in the hospital. After I signed the necessary paperwork, a nurse took me downstairs in a wheelchair, where my parents helped me into their car.

My mom had set up a temporary bed in the living room by covering a dark green couch from the seventies with sheets and pillows. For the first few days, everybody was very nice to me, but first thing Monday morning, I was left completely alone, in a dark house, lying on a green couch, crippled and unable to walk.

I tried for more than an hour to get off the couch by myself so that I could use the bathroom, but I couldn't. The couch was too low to the ground. There was no strength in my legs, and I couldn't bend my knees.

Every time I moved my left arm, pain from my broken collarbone shot through my shoulders. My other hand wasn't much help, because it was engulfed in a huge cast. It felt like my life was destroyed. I was hurting, angry, depressed and getting more negative and frustrated by the minute.

Eventually my mom came home. She helped me get

off the couch so that I could use the bathroom, but my anger continued to grow stronger by the minute. Every time I felt pain in my legs, it made me more and more angry.

My breaking point came a few days later when my mom was in the kitchen working. I was trying to get off the couch by myself, but it was just too painful. All I could do was lie halfway off in agonizing pain. All of a sudden, something inside of me snapped. A total rage of power came over me. I grabbed the back of a chair and forced myself to get up.

I was so driven, I couldn't feel the pain anymore. The strength that came over me laughed at the pain. I wanted to walk! I was so driven to walk, I didn't care if my pathetic, weak knees were torn off in the process. I would have walked on their bloody stumps.

After I blasted myself off the couch, I staggered straight legged through the kitchen. My mom started screaming. I walked past her and shoved the screen door open. I didn't know where I was going or what I was doing. I hobbled through the backyard, and made three circles around the apple tree in the center of the yard before coming back inside.

At first I didn't give God much credit, but he supernaturally healed my body that day. He also changed my attitude, because if I could walk once, I could do it again. Instead of feeling helpless and defeated, I felt empowered. I was so motivated that within a week, I was able to climb behind the wheel of an automobile and drive myself around town.

Today, I am in perfect health. I am able to run,

hike, bike, climb mountains and work construction. If I had allowed the doctors to cut into my knees, drill through my bones, and weave my tendons through the holes, I could still be lying on my parents' couch, crippled for life.

At the time of the car crash, I was only 20 years old. I didn't know a lot about God, and I didn't have a great relationship with him. I knew God was real and that he had miraculously saved my life from total destruction.

I had started praying from the time my car flipped upside down, and I continued praying while I lay on the pavement with the wind knocked out of me. I didn't understand the power of faith or how to use the power of faith to tap into God's healing power. I just did it! Faith is not a mental belief. Faith is putting your mental belief into action!

If I truly believe that God loves me, and that God takes no pleasure in seeing me crippled for life, and that God desires to make me whole, then all I need to do is ask God to heal me, believe that he has heard my prayer, and then put my faith into action by rising up off the couch.

When God looks down from heaven and sees me putting into action what I have already asked for, it opens up a spiritual conduit that allows God's healing power to flow into my life. As soon as I put my faith into action, God's healing power was released, my legs received supernatural strength, and I recovered.

If I had waited on the couch for God to miraculously heal my body, I would still be lying there. If I wanted all the pain to stop before I accepted God's healing power, all the muscles in my legs would have deteriorated from lack of use. The longer I would have lay on the couch, the worse my condition would have grown.

Faith, when put into action, opens the pipeline for God's healing power to flow into your life. If you never put your faith into action, then your faith is powerless. The apostle James says, *"faith without works is dead."*[2] In other words, faith without action is also dead.

If you believe that God wants to restore you and you accept his healing power by putting your faith into action, then God will be more empowered to work with your situation. If you sit around believing the disease is more powerful than God, and that your situation is hopeless, then your lack of faith will hinder God's healing from flowing into your body.

Another good example of how to put your faith into action comes from the Gospel of Luke. After Jesus entered a village, ten lepers started calling out to him saying, *"Jesus, Master, have mercy on us!"*[3]

When Jesus saw them, he said, *"Go and show yourselves to the priests."*[4]

Immediately, the men's faith started to rise. They had finally met Jesus—the master miracle worker, whom everybody was talking about. Jesus told them to show themselves to the priests. That meant he wanted them to follow the purification laws prescribed for letting lepers back into society.

The only problem was these men were covered with

highly contagious sores. They were not allowed any-where near the temple area. They couldn't even go into the town without running the risk of being stoned by an angry mob. They had to live in the deserted areas and ring a bell, or cry out with a loud voice, *unclean, unclean!*

Were these men going to believe in their disease? Or were they going to believe more in Jesus' desire to see them made whole? If Jesus said go, were they going to put their faith into action and expect Jesus to do what he promised on the journey? Or would they sit around and wait for the leprosy to leave their bodies before embarking on the journey?

If they looked at the sores and believed the disease was more powerful than Jesus, they never would have left the village. If they never did what Jesus told them to do, they would have never received the healing power of God.

After thinking about their situation, all ten men made a decision for Christ. They packed up a few belongings and set out for Jerusalem still covered with highly contagious sores. *And as they went, they were made clean.*[5]

When one of the men saw that he had been healed, he turned around and went back to the village. He threw himself at the feet of Jesus and started thanking him. Jesus asked him, *"Were not ten made clean? But the other nine, where are they? Was none of them found to return and give praise to God except this foreigner?"*[6]

Then Jesus said to the man, *"Get up and go on your way; your faith has made you well."*[7]

Before the ten lepers were made whole, they had to ask Jesus for healing, and then they had to put their faith into action to receive his healing power. In the same way, before I could rise up off the couch, I had to ask God for healing, and then I had to put my faith into action, rise up and start walking.

If you are sick, take some time right now and put your faith into action. Start by centering yourself in a meditative style of prayer. Picture Jesus, the divine Physician, coming to visit you. Look him in the eyes. Talk with him as if he were standing right in front of you. Open up your heart to him. Invite his healing power into your body.

After you have accepted the Lord's healing power, start putting your faith into action. Start doing what you were not previously able to do. If you are lying crippled on a couch, force yourself up and start walking in the name, power and authority of Jesus.

If you are unable to move your arm, raise it right now. If you can't bend over, start by touching your toes. If you have problems with your lungs, take a deep breath.

If you believe Jesus has the power to heal you, put your faith into action and receive his healing power. Allow the miracle-working power of God to flow into your body right now.

5

The Power of Salvation

In the Old Covenant, when a man committed a sin, he was allowed to pass the death penalty for his sinful actions onto a sacrificial lamb. After the lamb was slaughtered, the animal's blood made atonement for the man's sins.

This temporary system of repentance worked great for a time, but soon the people's hearts grew hardened. They were constantly committing sins and constantly performing purification rituals in the temple. No one was striving after holiness, and everybody was slaughtering animals to atone for their sins.

Because God desired more holiness from his children, he sent his only begotten Son into the world to take the place of the sacrificial lamb. The Son of God took on human flesh and became man. He lived a sinless life and demonstrated the Father's love through his actions.

On the night he was betrayed, Jesus completed the Passover meal with his disciples. He took bread and after blessing it, he broke it and said, *"This is my body, which is given for you. Do this in remembrance of me."*[1] Then he took the cup and after blessing it he said, *"This is my blood of the covenant, which is poured out for many for the forgiveness of sins.*"[2]

After this Jesus turned his body over to be tortured and crucified. Several guards stripped him of his clothes and tied his hands to a post above his head. Another guard took a whip made of leather cords that had sharp pieces of bone and rocks attached to their ends. The guard inflicted the full force of the whip across Jesus' back, shoulders and legs.

At first the sharp objects cut through the Lord's flesh. Then every time the guard brought the whip back for another assault, more and more of his flesh was torn away. It shredded his muscles and exposed his bones. Jesus' eyes were filled with tears, yet he continued to look at the men with love in his heart.

Finally, the guards untied Jesus and allowed his weak and bloody body to slump against the post. They threw a robe across his shoulders and placed a stick in his hand for a scepter. They mocked him, saying, *"Hail, King of the Jews!" They spat on him, and took the reed and struck him on the head.*[3]

After mocking Jesus, the guards stripped off the robe and tied a heavy cross to his shoulders. They forced him to begin the painful journey bearing the full weight of the cross. Every time Jesus fell, another sting of the whip cut into his flesh. Eventually, he reached Golgotha, the Place of the Skull, where they crucified him.

Suddenly darkness covered the whole earth. All the sins of mankind fell upon Jesus. The Father had to turn away. Jesus cried out with a loud voice, *"My God, my God, why have you forsaken me?"*[4] Jesus became the sacrificial Lamb of God. He paid humanity's price for our sins, the penalty of death, with his own blood.

Afterward there was a major shift in the spiritual realm. The curtain in the temple was torn in two. The earth shook. Rocks split. Tombs were opened, and many bodies of the saints who had fallen asleep were raised. Satan never expected it to happen, but three days later, Jesus rose from the dead and established the New Covenant.

This is the Gospel message, and before you will be able to tap into its power, you will first need to accept the Lord's sacrifice on the cross for the forgiveness of your sins. You can do this right now by taking some time and centering yourself in prayer.

Have you ever turned your back on God and believed Satan's lies over God's goodness? If so, the penalty for disobedience or any other type of sin is death. If you have committed the slightest sin, no matter how small, are you willing to pay the death penalty yourself? Or do you want Jesus to pay the penalty on your behalf?

If you want Jesus to pay the penalty on your behalf, picture the Lord lying before you as he is being nailed to the cross. Picture him having a hard time breathing as he suffers the agonizing pain. Look him in the eyes and thank him for paying the death penalty on your behalf. Go through your entire life and confess all your sins to him. Symbolically take all your sins, all the people you have hurt, directly and indirectly, and offer them to Jesus.

Give Jesus all of your sins. He has the power to pay the death penalty on your behalf. He has already paid the price. He loves you. Give him all your sins. Look him in the eyes and make a promise that you will do everything in your power from here on out to avoid sin at all cost. Make a promise to avoid all kinds of temptation and to utterly reject and forsake evil. Close your prayer with anything else you would like to say to the Lord.

Before you will be able to accept the full power of the Gospel message, you will need to understand why Jesus suffered the cruelty of the whip. Jesus didn't need to have his flesh shredded by soldiers. God could have easily protected his Son from the scourging at the pillar, in the same way that God protected him from having his bones broken on the cross:

The soldiers came and broke the legs of the first and of the other who had been crucified with him. But when they came to Jesus and saw that he was already dead, they did not break his legs. Instead, one of the soldiers pierced his side with a spear, and at once blood and water came out. These things occurred so that the scripture might be fulfilled, "None of his bones shall be broken." And again another passage of scripture says, "They will look on the one whom they have pierced."[5]

If God was able to protect the Sacrificial Lamb so that none of his bones were broken, then surely God could have protected Jesus from suffering the cruelty of the whip.

Jesus suffered the cruelty of the whip because he wanted to take the sickness of humanity onto his own flesh, so that you could be healed.

> *Yet it was our infirmities that he bore,*
> *our sufferings that he endured,*
> *While we thought of him as stricken,*
> *as one smitten by God and afflicted.*
> *But he was pierced for our offenses,*
> *crushed for our sins,*
> *Upon him was the chastisement that makes us whole,*
> *by his stripes we were healed.*[6]

Jesus endured the cruelty of the whip so that you could be healed. He was completely innocent of all sin, yet he willingly chose to take every kind of sickness and disease upon his own body, so that you could have healing and wholeness in yours. *By his wounds you have been healed.*[7]

The price to forgive your sins and the price to heal your infirmities has already been paid. Jesus paid for both so that you could be set free. The power to forgive men's sins and the power to heal men's bodies are inseparable. They both come from Jesus. You can make a choice to have your sins forgiven, just as you can make a choice to have your body healed.

Don't think you are doing Jesus a favor by bearing your own infirmities. They will only kill you. They will rob you of your strength, energy, finances and service unto the Lord. Jesus wants you to be made whole, so that you can serve him with all your strength. Jesus wants you to be healthy and strong, so that you can proclaim the Gospel message for the entire world to hear.

The healing power is already here. The price has

already been paid. All you need to do is tap into the Lord's healing power by accepting the Gospel message. The healing power of Christ will be allowed to flow into your life as soon as you accept the sacrifice that Jesus made on your behalf.

If you are in need of Jesus' healing power, you may want to take some time right now and center yourself in a meditative style of prayer. Picture Jesus bound in chains with his hands tied above his head. Picture a soldier lashing the whip across his back without mercy. Look into his loving eyes. Allow his love for you to well up in your heart. He is enduring this hardship so that you can be healed.

If your love compels you, step in front of the soldier and allow your body to shield Jesus' body from the whip. Allow yourself to feel the sickness of evil as it is being inflicted across his backside. When you have suffered all the sickness that your humanity can bear, allow yourself to move through Jesus' body. Pass through him and leave behind your sickness and disease. As you pass through Jesus' body, take with you his enduring love and strength.

Leave your old, crippled body parts behind, and take Jesus' new strong body parts with you. Allow the strength of Jesus' body to flow through your body. Allow the Lord's blood to wash through your veins and free you from every kind of genetic and cellular disorder.

After you have passed through the body of Jesus and are made perfectly clean, start putting your faith into action. Start doing whatever it is that you have been prevented from doing in the past. Allow the power of the Gospel message to transform your life today.

6

The Power of Command

I had been drifting in and out of sleep all night. At first, I couldn't tell if the noises were real or if they were coming from a dream. I could see a picture of myself standing on a staircase. I started hearing construction noises. The sounds grew louder.

Then I could see a window in the distance covered with flies. The noise of the insects grew louder. All of a sudden, I could feel my spirit-man coming under attack. A paralyzing evil force had come over me.

I wasn't dreaming anymore. This was a real live demonic attack. I was fully awake and trying to break free by speaking the name of Jesus. I tried with all my strength, but I could barely say the Lord's name. I tried again and again, but the evil force had a powerful grip on me.

I had to fight with all my strength to say the name of Jesus. Every time I invoked the Lord's name my words grew stronger and stronger. Finally, I could give the command with full authority, *I bind you Satan in the name of Jesus.* By then the paralyzing grip had already left, and my spirit-man was fired up to the point where it was very easy for me to start singing praises to God.

I have only experienced two demonic dreams in my life. One occurred when I was learning about spiritual warfare, and the other happened right before I embarked on my first missions trip. Both experiences lasted less than a minute, because I already knew how to break free—by invoking the powerful name of Jesus.

Right before the disciples set out for their first missionary trip, Jesus called them together and *gave them power and authority over all demons and to cure diseases, and he sent them out to proclaim the kingdom of God and to heal.*[1]

After the disciples departed, they went through the villages, *bringing the good news and curing diseases everywhere.*[2] Soon after, Jesus appointed seventy others and sent them to every town and village with the same instructions—*cure the sick who are there, and say to them, "The kingdom of God has come near to you."*[3]

When Jesus sent these men and women forth, they became ambassadors for Christ. They went to every town and village representing the Lord. When they spoke, they were speaking as the Lord's official representatives. When they invoked the Lord's name, they were invoking the Lord's power.

When the disciples returned from their trip and reported to Jesus all the miraculous signs and wonders they had performed, they were filled with great joy and said, *"Lord, in your name even the demons submit to us!"*[4]

The Lord said, *"I watched Satan fall from heaven like a flash of lightning. See, I have given you authority to tread on snakes and scorpions, and over all the power of the enemy; and nothing will hurt you."*[5]

The same power has been given to all disciples—all you need to do is start using it. By invoking the Lord's name, the Lord's power will be manifested in your life. Once the Lord's power is manifested, all you need to do is direct it toward a worthy ministry purpose or recipient.

A good example on how to use the power of the command comes from the Book of Acts. When Peter went to Lydda, he found a paralyzed man named Aeneas who had been bedridden for eight years. After Peter told him about the Gospel message, he invoked the name, power and authority of Jesus by saying to the man, *"Jesus Christ heals you; get up and make your bed!" And immediately he got up. And all the residents of Lydda and Sharon saw him and turned to the Lord.*[6]

When Peter invoked the name of Jesus, the healing power of Jesus was made available. Peter then united the healing power of Jesus with a command by saying, *Get up and make your bed!* Before the healing power was allowed to flow into the paralyzed man's life, Aeneas had to follow the command that was spoken to him. He had to put his faith into action, stand up and make his bed.

To help the disciples learn how to use the power of a command more efficiently, Jesus taught them a valuable lesson one day by saying, *"Truly I tell you, if you say to this mountain, 'Be taken up and thrown into the sea,' and if you do not doubt in your heart, but believe that what you say will come to pass, it will be done for you."*[7]

In order for the power of the command to take effect, the disciples had to speak to the mountain. They had to address the mountain by name and give it a command. Notice Jesus says, if you *say* to the mountain, it will be done for you. Not if you *pray* about the mountain being moved for you.

The Lord demonstrated the power of the command when he stopped by Peter's mother-in-law's house. After ministering to a large crowd of people all day, the disciples were hungry. They wanted to stop by Peter's mother-in-law's house on their way home, but unfortunately when they arrived, they found her lying sick in bed.

Immediately Jesus went to her bedside. He *stood over her and rebuked the fever, and it left her. Immediately she got up and began to serve them.*[8]

Before Peter's mother-in-law could be healed, Jesus had to rebuke the fever. He addressed the fever by name, condemning it for its actions, and he told it to get out of her body. He commanded the fever to leave, and afterward the sickness left her body.

The apostle Paul also used the power of the command when he was preaching the Gospel to the people in Lystra. After he had finished speaking, he noticed *a man sitting who could not use his feet and had never walked, for he had been crippled from birth.*[9]

Paul, looking at him intently and seeing that he had faith to be healed, said in a loud voice, "Stand upright on your feet."[10]

The man sprang up and began to walk.[11]

Paul did not pray for the man's healing. He gave a command. Paul was acting as an ambassador for Christ.

After he preached the Gospel message on the Lord's behalf, he gave a command, and the healing power of Jesus was made available. When the crippled man put his faith into action, the Lord's healing power entered his body, and he was made whole.

When I first learned about the power of the command, I was hiking in the Colorado mountains after a snowstorm. A foot of fresh powder had fallen the night before, and everything was covered with a peaceful, sparkling-white glow.

As I proceeded slowly down a steep slope near a running stream, I slipped on some ice. I came crashing down and twisted my leg. Immediately, I grabbed my knee and started praying. After rising to my feet and brushing the snow off my clothes, I proceeded down the mountain.

I could tell my knee suffered some kind of injury, but it appeared to be working fine, so I tried not to think about it and kept walking. Eventually, the swelling went away, but every so often a low-level pain would come and go.

Having learned about the power of the command, I decided to give it a try. I laid my hands on my knee and said, *I rebuke you, pain, in the name of Jesus, and I command you to get out of my body!* Immediately, the pain left.

Over the next several weeks, the pain came back about eight more times. Every time the pain appeared, I either rebuked it in the name of Jesus, or I reminded myself that I had already been healed. Every time I did, the pain left my body.

If you are in need of God's healing power, take some time right now and invoke the name of the Lord. Lay your hands on whatever area of your body that needs healing and command the sickness to leave. If you are suffering from a medical illness like Peter's mother-in-law, address the illness by name and command it to get out of your body in the name of Jesus.

If you are under attack from demonic spirits of infirmity, command them to get out of your body in the name, power and authority of Jesus. If you are suffering from back pain, command your spine to come into perfect alignment. If you are suffering from a genetic disease, command every cell in your body to come into complete electrical and chemical balance in Jesus' name. Invoke the name that is above every other name, and allow the healing power of Jesus to transform your life right now.

7

The Power of Prayer

Brittany was lying on the floor covered with blankets, waiting for us to pray with her. She was only six years old and suffered from terrible arthritic attacks in her legs. She would often wake up in the middle of the night screaming because the pain was so intense.

Her mother had the same condition. Vanessa came from a Muslim and Hindu background where eight of her twelve brothers and sisters had committed suicide. She knew we were dealing with generational curses, because the Lord had already started showing her how the sins of her parents were being passed down to the third and fourth generations.

As we gathered around Brittany to pray, she pulled the blanket over her head. I sat down on the floor next to her, and her mother, along with another woman, took a seat on the couch.

We began by asking the Lord to show us how to pray. After a moment of silence, Vanessa said, "Lord, please heal my daughter. Please make it go away. I don't want to give her any more Tylenol. Please heal her legs so that she won't hurt anymore."

"Yes, Lord," I said. "Please have mercy on

Vanessa's parents and grandparents. Please forgive all their sins. We ask you to visit them right now, wherever they are, and give them the opportunity to choose you as their Lord and Savior. Please give them the opportunity to hear the Gospel message so that their sins may be forgiven."

"Yes Lord," Vanessa said. "I hold no resentment or bitterness toward any of my relatives, and I ask you to have mercy on my entire family lineage."

"We ask you, Lord, to put your cross between Vanessa and her parents," I said. "We take authority over all generationally inherited sins and curses, and we break them right now by the power of your name. We ask you to wash all her past generations with your blood and place your cross between Vanessa and her parents, and her grandparents, all the way back to the beginning of time.

"Please speak to Vanessa, Lord Jesus. Please open her ears to hear your voice. Please give her a word or a vision, or bring up a memory from her past. Whatever it is that she needs to hear, please speak it to your daughter right now."

After a long silence, Vanessa said, "I think he wants me to pray about the alcoholism."

"Good, let's go with that," I said.

"Please help my brother, Tomell," she said. "He is struggling so much right now. Please help him make the right choices for you."

"Yes, Lord, we hereby take authority over all spirits of alcoholism in Vanessa's family and we bind you, evil spirits, in the name of Jesus. We denounce the practice of poisoning our bodies. We ask you to send forth your holy warring angels and strike down and destroy all demonic spirits of alcoholism. We ask your holy warring angels to go forth right now and purify and cleanse Vanessa's entire family lineage."

"Yes Lord," Vanessa said.

After a long moment of silence, I placed my hand on Brittany's head. Her mother had been holding her tiny hand the entire time. As we continued to pray, I said, "We thank you, Lord, for breaking all generationally inherited curses that have come against Brittany. We hereby dedicate her to you for your service.

"We say that nothing evil can touch her or hurt her any longer. We hereby command anything evil or demonic that has been coming against her to get out of her body right now and never return.

"We hereby command all the cells, muscles, joints and genetic makeup in her body to be healed in the name, power and authority of Jesus. We command all the cells to come into perfect electrical and chemical balance in Jesus' name.

"Send down the fire of your Holy Spirit to come into her body and bring complete healing. We say to you, spirits of arthritis and pain in her legs, get out of her body in the name of Jesus and never return. Come, Holy Spirit, and fill Brittany with your healing power.

"Now Brittany, I want you to pray to Jesus. I want you to ask Jesus to heal you. Will you do that?"

The little girl was just lying on the floor smiling at me.

"Jesus loves little girls. Every time a little girl comes to Jesus for healing he takes away all her pain. Do you want Jesus to heal you so that your legs will stop hurting?"

Brittany just looked at me with her big brown eyes and started giggling.

"Maybe your mom could say the words, and you can repeat after her," I said.

"Yes, Brittany, come on, I want you to do this," Vanessa said. "Pray after me, Lord Jesus, please heal my legs."

"Jesus, please heal my legs," Brittany said.

After Brittany repeated all her mother's words, the Spirit of the Lord filled me with great joy. I knew Jesus healed his precious daughter at that moment because Brittany was completely innocent. She was too young to have brought on any kind of demonic illness through her own sins. It all came through the sins of her family lineage as described in the Book of Exodus:

You shall have no other gods before me. You shall not make for yourself an idol, whether in the form of anything that is in heaven above, or that is on the earth beneath, or that is in the water under the earth. You shall not bow down to them or worship them; for I the Lord your God am a jealous God, punishing children for the iniquity of parents, to the third and the fourth generation of those who reject me, but showing steadfast love to the thousandth generation of those who love me and keep my commandments.[1]

If Brittany's grandfather intentionally poisoned his body with alcohol and invited evil spirits into his body through false religious practices, then all kinds of demonic illnesses would have the right to enter his genetic makeup and make him sick. When Brittany's grandfather passed along his genetic makeup into his wife's womb, all his defective genes would be passed along to the future generations.

If Brittany's great-grandfather was involved with witchcraft or any other type of idolatry, he would have been making agreements with the devil through his religious practices. When the man died, the demons would not die with him; they would continue to live and simply follow the family lineage by moving on to the nearest relative who has also been influenced by the same conditioning.

If God allows our parents to pass along all their good traits, he also allows them to pass along all their bad traits. If your parents served the false god of money for many years, and you inherited a great fortune, you may have also inherited a spirit of greed and control along with the pride of your family's heritage.

It is through the power of prayer that God is able to show us these issues and help us break them. Prayer not only protects us from generationally inherited curses, but it also has the power to release God's blessings into our lives. There's a great amount of power in prayer, but the power does not come by repeating the same words over and over again.

Jesus says, *"When you are praying, do not heap up*

empty phrases as the Gentiles do; for they think that they will be heard because of their many words. Do not be like them, for your Father knows what you need before you ask him."[2]

If you are sick, you will not be able to buy your healing through the sheer multiplication of words. God hears the prayer requests of the saints on earth, just as clearly as he hears the intercession of the saints in heaven. It doesn't matter how many people you get to repeat the same prayer request over and over again. If the answer is no the first time, if will remain the same until you deal with the underlying issues.

The most effective way to pray for healing is to ask Jesus to show you the source of your illness. Once you have discovered the source, ask the Lord what needs to happen before you can be healed.

Prayer is a two-way conversation with God, similar to a telephone call where one person talks and the other person listens. After you make the connection by entering into God's presence, make your prayer request along with plenty of praise and worship.

Afterward, sit in silence and wait for God to speak to you. God desperately desires to speak to you. God is always trying to speak to his beloved children; the problem is, most people never take the time to listen, or they don't really want to hear what the Lord has to say.

If you are sick, tap into the power of prayer. Invoke the name of the Lord and have a conversation with the great Physician. Ask Jesus to show you the source of the sickness. Ask him to bring up any issues in your family lineage that may be allowing a curse or sickness to come against you.

If the Lord shows you that your great-grandfather practiced freemasonry, ask him if he wants you to acquire some deliverance prayers, so that you can pray more effectively. If the Lord shows you the sins of idolatry, alcoholism and witchcraft in your family lineage, take authority over these generationally inherited curses in the name, power and authority of Jesus.

You should be spending several hours a day communing with Jesus—the great lover of your soul. Tap into the power of prayer right now. Jesus deeply desires to set you free. He desperately desires to release you from all bondage. Turn to him right now, so that his miraculous healing power can start transforming your life today.

8

The Power of Forgiveness

When I first started practicing contemplative prayer, I made a commitment to spend an hour a day listening to the soft-spoken voice of the Lord. At the time, I was attending a church with a prayer chapel located inside of a large octagon room built out of glass blocks.

Even after spending a lot of time in the prayer chapel, I still had a hard time centering myself. All kinds of distracting thoughts would run through my mind from the day's events. It took a lot of practice, but eventually I was able to acquire the necessary discipline to hear from the Lord.

There were many days when God would fill my heart with his peaceful presence. Other times he would bring up a hurtful event from my past. At first, I didn't know how to deal with these negative experiences. It felt like they were interrupting my quiet time with the Lord. I tried to shove them back down. Then I realized the Lord was bringing them up because he wanted me to forgive some people from my past.

In the second Book of Corinthians, Paul talks about the lack of forgiveness as one of Satan's devices. He says, "I do not want you to be *outwitted by Satan* or to be *ignorant of his designs.*" He also warns us, *"Do not let the sun go down on your anger, and do not make room for the devil."*[2]

After spending a lot of time practicing contemplative prayer, I realized I had to go back and forgive the man who caused my auto accident. The driver who cut me off caused a lot of damage to my life. My car was totally destroyed and my legs were almost crippled for life.

If I made a choice not to forgive him and started dwelling on the damage, the devil could have entered my thoughts and fueled my anger. The more distorted my thinking would have grown, the harder my heart would have become, until eventually I would have cut myself off from God's graces and healing power.

I am very fortunate because at the time of the accident, I did everything in my power to receive God's graces and allow them to flow into my life. On the second day of my hospitalization, I asked the nurse if I could see a priest, because I wanted to go to confession. Instead, they sent me a non-denominational chaplain. I was so desperate to get myself back in right relationship with God, that I made my confession to the man right there in the hospital room.

Afterward a nurse mentioned that the lady who was driving the school bus was on the same floor, a few doors down. After thinking about it, I asked the nurse if I could go to her room and see her. The nurse agreed, and they put me in a wheelchair. She rolled me down the hall and into the woman's room. After introducing myself, I apologized for involving her with the accident.

She didn't say much in response, and I was only in her room for a brief moment. I don't know if my apologies helped the lady feel any better, but it helped my heart to open up and allow God's healing power to flow into my life.

If my heart was not open to God's love, I could have very easily continued to feed my anger, and it would have turned into bitterness and eventually a hateful attitude toward life. The more I would have fed into the lies and devices of the devil, the harder my heart would have grown, until I would have been completely cut off from God's graces. If I would have cut my heart off from God through the sin of anger and lack of forgiveness, I could still be lying on my parents' couch to this very day.

Even though I received God's healing graces, and my legs were miraculously restored within a few weeks, I still had to go back and forgive the driver who caused the accident. Just because my body made a miraculous recovery doesn't mean all the anger and resentment in my heart instantly disappeared.

To work my way through the forgiveness process, I had to go back in time and re-create the accident scene to the best of my ability. In my imagination I pictured the silver sports car blocking my lane of traffic. The bus came to a skidding halt across both southbound lanes of traffic. After my car was flipped upside down and spun through the air, it came crashing down near the median.

After inviting Jesus to join me, I entered the scene and rushed over and ministered to the young man who was lying on the pavement. He couldn't move, and he had the wind knocked out of him. He was lying next to his car looking up at the front tire. I put my arms around the young man and began to pray with him. I reassured him that he would survive this tragedy with incredible strength. He was overjoyed to see that Jesus had come on the scene to be with him. I held the young man in my arms, as Jesus laid his healing hands on him. Afterward I spoke many blessings into his life. I waited there with him until the ambulance arrived.

After the paramedics put him on the stretcher, I ran over to the school bus and ministered to the bus driver in the same way. The motor and transmission had pinned her inside the cab. I continued to speak reassuring words to her until the rescue crew came and cut the door open for her to get out.

After the paramedics took her away in the ambulance, I knew it was time to deal with the driver of the silver sports car. I still had a lot of anger at the man who had cut me off. I read from the police report that he had been drinking. A part of me wanted to pull him out of his car window and beat him in full view of the crowd that had gathered.

As I approached his car, I asked Jesus for the grace to release all my anger and hurt feelings. Instead of looking at him like an irresponsible drunk who didn't care about anyone or anything except himself, I started looking at him with compassion.

I started seeing him through the Lord's eyes of mercy and grace. I could see that he had tears of sorrow welling up in his eyes. He was scared to death. He didn't want any of this to happen. In my imagination, the man started to cry. I broke down and hugged him. We both needed the Lord's love. Jesus walked over and laid his hands on our shoulders and filled us with his healing power.

After God's love flowed through my heart and into the life of the man who had caused the accident, I knew the forgiveness process was complete. I said good-bye to him and closed the meditative prayer time by saying the Lord's Prayer.

Our Father in heaven, hallowed be your name. Your kingdom come. Your will be done, on earth as it is in heaven. Give us this day our daily bread. And forgive us our debts, as we also have forgiven our debtors. And do not bring us to the time of trial, but rescue us from the evil one.[3]

After I said the prayer, I realized the Lord wanted me to experience the fullness of his heavenly Father's blessings. In heaven there is no sickness, disease or death. There is only pure light, love, truth, holiness and worship. When we pray the Lord's Prayer, we are asking the Father to send down all the heavenly blessings that we need on earth. *Your will be done, on earth as it is in heaven.[4]*

Heaven has an abundance of everything we need. For every sickness on earth, there's an entire storehouse of heavenly blessings waiting to be released. For every financial problem, there's an abundance of wisdom. For every personal problem, there's an abundance of fortitude.

When we pray the Lord's Prayer, we are asking the Father to send forth his blessings on earth, as they exist in heaven. We are praying for everything on earth to be made like everything in heaven. Because God wants to fulfill his part of the prayer, all we need to do is fulfill our part of the prayer.

In almost all the words of the Lord's Prayer, we are asking for something. We are asking for God's abundant resources from heaven to flow into our lives. We ask him for our daily bread. We ask him for protection from the evil one. We ask to be forgiven for our sins. There's only one part of this prayer where God asks something from us: *forgive us our debts, as we also have forgiven our debtors.*[5]

This is so important that Jesus says, *"For if you forgive others their trespasses, your heavenly Father will also forgive you; but if you do not forgive others, neither will your Father forgive your trespasses."*[6]

If you are suffering a serious illness, the lack of forgiveness has the ability to prevent God's healing power from flowing into your life. God wants to set you free from all sickness and disease. It is God's will that your life on earth be similar to your future life in heaven. God wants you to live in pure love, truth, light and holiness. God wants to open up the storehouses of heaven and flood your life with his abundant blessings.

You can tap into the power of forgiveness right now by turning to Jesus in prayer. If he brings up a hurtful past event, you may need to deal with it before the Lord's healing power will be allowed to flow into your body.

The forgiveness process begins by an act of your will. You will need to make a choice to forgive the person who hurt you. You will need to surrender all your pain and the damage that you experienced to the Lord. After you release everything negative and harmful, you will need to accept the Lord's love, and allow his love to flow through your heart into the person's life that hurt you.

If you are in need of physical healing, and the Lord has already shown you some areas of your past where forgiveness is required, take some time right now in prayer. Find a quiet place in your home or at church. Invite Jesus to go back into your past and allow his love to enter into the time when you were injured. Go back and minister to that hurt little boy or girl from your childhood.

You will need to find a way to minister to the person who hurt you. Try looking at them through the eyes of Jesus' love and compassion. Try to see how they are hurting themselves. Allow Jesus' love to fill your heart as you speak the necessary words, "I forgive you."

If any kind of evil thoughts or feelings of anger are preventing you from fully forgiving the person, take authority over any demonic spirits in the name, power and authority of Jesus. Say the words out loud and with great authority, *I bind you spirits of anger and resentment in the name of Jesus.*

If you have picked up any kind of sexual spirits of perversion from a person who hurt you, bind them in the name of Jesus. Command any demonic spirits to get out of your body and to never again return. Afterward, have Jesus lay his healing hands on you and wash you clean.

Keep working on all your traumatic past experiences until you bring them to completion. Ask the Lord to show you anything else that needs to be denounced or forgiven. Keep working on everything the Lord shows you until you are completely filled with God's love.

When God's love can flow through your heart and into the life of the person who hurt you, the forgiveness process is complete. When God's love can freely flow through your heart, God's healing power will also start flowing through your body.

9

The Power of God's Word

Many years ago I met a homeless woman named Amber. During the summer months, she would sleep outside underneath a large commercial sign next to a chain-link fence. The guard dogs on the other side of the fence would keep her company at night by curling up beside her to keep her warm.

Over the years I helped Amber acquire several jobs and rented many hotel rooms on her behalf. At one point she was able to move into her own apartment, but within a few months, she was evicted. Amber was an alcoholic, and every time she stopped drinking, her sobriety would last for a short time, and then she would end up back on the streets.

One day I received a phone call from the house manager at the Rescue Mission. I could feel the panic in his voice as he said, "Amber was attacked last night. Apparently she had been arguing with some guys earlier that day. We think one of them came back at night and tried to kill her when she was sleeping."

"Oh no! Is she okay?"

"The perpetrator used a cinder block. Amber lay unconscious all night wrapped up in a bloody blanket.

The guys who found her said they could see her brain exposed through the large gash in her skull."

"Where is she now?" I asked.

"After we called the police, the paramedics took her away early this morning. I tried contacting several hospitals, but no one would give me any information."

"Thanks for letting me know," I said.

After getting off the phone with the man, I immediately started calling around. It took about an hour, but eventually I found a woman named Jane Doe who had been admitted for head trauma at Denver General.

After I arrived at the intensive care unit, several security guards escorted me to Jane Doe's room. The police were still looking for suspects. They wanted to make sure nobody would come back to cause her anymore harm.

Upon entering her room, I could barely recognize Amber. Her face was swollen, and her nose was broken. She had black and blue marks underneath both eyes. The nurses had shaved her head so surgeons could repair the trauma to her skull. The heavy black stitches they used looked like train tracks running across the side of her head in a semicircular pattern.

I started feeling sick when I noticed there was a tube attached to the center of her cranium with shinny brass fittings. The nurse said it was helping to prevent pressure from building up inside her head. There were many other tubes connected to her body, including one from a breathing respirator. The nurse said she had removed the respirator twice to see if Amber could breathe on her own, but both times she failed the test.

All during this time I had been praying, *"Oh God, please help Amber,"* but deep in my heart I lacked the spiritual strength to pray effectively. No one thought Amber was going to live, and before long, I started preparing myself for the worst-case scenario.

To make matters worse, I felt guilty for the way I had left Amber the last time I'd seen her. I was dropping off some paperwork a few weeks prior. She was standing on the sidewalk waiting for me, but after spending more than a year trying to help her, I had given up hope. I felt like I was wasting my time. I was mad at myself and disappointed with her progress, so after handing Amber the papers, I drove off in an impatient rush. I could hear her calling out to me from the sidewalk, "Wait Rob... Rob."

As I stood in the hospital room looking at Amber, I felt terrible and partly responsible. All I could do was stop by and visit her to see how she was doing, but every day her condition got worse. There was a terrible stench of death in the room, and the doctors wanted to insert a long-term feeding tube into her stomach.

I continued to pray for Amber, but my prayers lacked the necessary power of faith. I didn't think Amber would live, and my negative attitude was hindering my ability to pray for a miraculous recovery. To make matters worse, my heart was hardened. A part of me didn't want to see Amber back on the streets, causing more problems and continuing her lifestyle of drunken debauchery.

Eventually, I was able to work through my negative

attitude and get back into my heart. A few days later, a lady from my Bible study group offered to go with me to the hospital and pray for Amber. We were able to pray with love in our hearts. We interceded on her behalf and asked God to forgive all her sins. I took a bottle of anointing oil along, and when the nurses weren't looking, I anointed Amber's head and hands.

After we anointed Amber with oil and prayed the prayer of faith with love in our hearts, Amber started to recover. The next day she regained consciousness and began breathing on her own. A few days later, she could sit up in a wheelchair by herself. Within two weeks, she was strong enough to start fighting with the nurses. On several occasions, the medical staff had to sedate her and strap her to the bed, because she tried to leave the hospital with the feeding tube still attached to her stomach.

Six months later, Amber had made a complete recovery. God worked a profound miracle, and all we needed to do to access the Lord's healing power was follow the simple instructions contained in Sacred Scripture: *Whatever you ask for in prayer with faith, you will receive.*[1]

Before God's healing power could be released into Amber's life, someone needed to believe that her situation was *not* hopeless. Someone needed to believe that God had the power, desire and love to restore Amber to perfect health.

It was also necessary for two or more Spirit-filled believers to come together in agreement before God's miracle-working power could be released. Jesus says,

"Again, truly I tell you, if two of you agree on earth about anything you ask, it will be done for you by my Father in heaven. For where two or three are gathered in my name, I am there among them."[2]

In the same way that God healed Amber, he also wants to heal all his beloved children. All you need to do is follow the simple instructions contained in Sacred Scripture. A good example of how to apply the power of God's healing promise to your life comes from the Book of James:

Are any among you sick? They should call for the elders of the church and have them pray over them, anointing them with oil in the name of the Lord. The prayer of faith will save the sick, and the Lord will raise them up; and anyone who has committed sins will be forgiven. Therefore confess your sins to one another, and pray for one another, so that you may be healed.[3]

1. Call on Spirit-filled elders to pray with you.
2. Have them anoint you with oil.
3. Pray the prayer of faith with the elders.
4. Make an intensive search of your past and confess all sinfulness.

If you do everything God's Word tells you to do, you can expect God to answer your prayer request exactly as you have spoken it from deep within the recesses of your heart. All you need is faith the size of a mustard seed, and you will be able to say to the mountain, *"Move from here to there,"* and it will move; and *nothing will be impossible for you.[4]*

What are you waiting for? God's promise of healing is for you. Call upon Spirit-filled believers to pray with you. Tap into the power of faith and stand firm on the promises contained in Sacred Scripture. Allow the Lord's miracle-working power to transform your life today.

10

The Power of God's Calling

One day Jesus entered the synagogue on the Sabbath day. When he stood up to give the reading, someone handed him a scroll from the prophet Isaiah. He unrolled it and said, *"The Spirit of the Lord is upon me, because he has anointed me to bring good news to the poor. He has sent me to proclaim release to the captives and recovery of sight to the blind, to let the oppressed go free, to proclaim the year of the Lord's favor.*[1]

After he rolled up the scroll, he gave it back to the attendant and said, *"Today this scripture has been fulfilled in your hearing."*[2]

Jesus fulfilled the words of this prophecy all throughout his ministry and in the same way, he has called all Christians to participate in his healing and deliverance ministry. He sent us forth to accomplish the same works that he accomplished when he said, *"Very truly, I tell you, the one who believes in me will also do the works that I do and, in fact, will do greater works than these, because I am going to the Father."*[3]

Jesus has offered this invitation to all believers. All you need to do is surrender your life into the Lord's service and start walking in complete obedience. When you start walking the walk as Jesus did, God will start using you to advance his kingdom here on earth.

A good example of this is demonstrated in the lives of the disciples. *Stephen, full of grace and power, did great wonders and signs among the people.*[4]

Peter's shadow has enough power to heal people. *They even carried out the sick into the streets, and laid them on cots and mats, in order that Peter's shadow might fall on some of them as he came by.*[5]

God did extraordinary miracles through Paul, so that when the handkerchiefs or aprons that had touched his skin were brought to the sick, their diseases left them, and the evil spirits came out of them.[6]

In the same way that God worked many powerful miracles through the lives of the disciples, he also wants to use you to advance his kingdom here on earth. He wants to fill you with the power of his Holy Spirit, so that you can start performing the same signs and wonders the Lord promised to all believers:

And these signs will accompany those who believe: by using my name they will cast out demons; they will speak in new tongues; they will pick up snakes in their hands, and if they drink any deadly thing, it will not hurt them; they will lay their hands on the sick, and they will recover.[7]

When the Lord said, *"Go into all the world and pro-claim the good news to the whole creation,"*[8] he actually wants us to share the Gospel message with all nations. When we step out in faith and start performing the works of ministry that have been assigned to us, God will back up our words and prayer requests with his miracle-working power.

A good example of this comes from a healing crusade in West Africa. After the Gospel message had been proclaimed, God sent forth his healing power and hundreds of lives were changed. One man was so excited that he kept running back and forth on the platform waving his cane in the air. He displayed an incredible amount of love and joy as he described how the Lord healed his arthritic condition.

Another middle-aged man named Princeworth had been involved in an automobile accident. When the car hit him it almost severed his right foot. His ankle and lower leg bone were completely crushed. He had just spent six months in the hospital undergoing three different operations, but he was still unable to walk.

During the prayer time, Princeworth was sitting on the grass next to his crutches. When we prayed for healing, the vast crowd started putting their faith into action. The sea of people started swarming, some were jumping, others were waving their arms around and moving back and forth.

When Princeworth saw all the excitement, he started crying out for someone to help him stand up. The man next to him grabbed his hands and pulled him to his feet. Instantly his pain was gone, and he was able to walk. After sharing his testimony the first night, he came back the following evening to say, "I was able to walk all day without using my crutches."

Another man named Edmond was totally blind in

his right eye. He was diagnosed with glaucoma, and the increasing pressures in his left eye made it almost impossible for him to see. When we prayed for healing, Edmond covered his eyes with his hands. When he removed them, he started jumping for joy, because he could see again.

Another man named Jonas had severe stiffness in both knees. It wasn't possible for him to kneel or bend his legs without a lot of pain. When we prayed for healing, Jonas put his hands on his waist, because he was also experiencing a terrible discomfort in his left hip socket. He said, "I could feel a warm heat running through my body and down my legs."

Even though the illness left his body the first evening, Jonas wanted to wait until the third night before giving his testimony. He wanted to make sure the healing was real. As I watched him squat down in front of me, and rise again like a limber child, I assured him that the Lord's healing power was very real.

What are you waiting for? The Lord needs your help. Jesus cannot lay hands on other people without your assistance. God has chosen you to change the world. He wants to create a divine ministry partnership with you. He wants to fill you with his miracle-working power, so that you can minister his healing touch to all the nations of the world.

The time is now—the kingdom of heaven is at hand!

Notes

Introduction
1. Genesis 1:26.
2. Genesis 2:18.
3. Genesis 4:7.
4. Revelation 12:9.
5. Exodus 15:26.
6. Ezekiel 36:25–28.

1 – The Power of Desire
1. John 5:6.
2. John 5:7.
3. John 5:8.
4. James 1:5–8.

2 – The Power of Truth
1. Luke 13:11.
2. Luke 13:12–13.
3. Luke 13:16.
4. John 8:32.

3 – The Power of Belief
1. Mark 5:26.
2. Mark 5:28.
3. Mark 5:30.
4. Mark 5:31.
5. Mark 5:33.
6. Mark 5:34.
7. Hebrews 11:6.
8. Matthew 9:27.
9. Matthew 9:28.
10. Matthew 9:28.
11. Matthew 9:29–30.
12. Matthew 15:22.
13. Matthew 15:24.
14. Matthew 15:28.
15. Matthew 15:28.
16. Job 1:1.
17. Job 1:8.
18. Job 1:9–11.
19. Job 1:12.
20. Job 2:3.

21. Job 2:4–5.
22. Job 2:6.
23. Job 2:7.
24. Luke 11:14.
25. Matthew 17:17–18.

4 – The Power of Faith
1. Accident photo by Lakewood police department.
2. NAB James 2:26.
3. Luke 17:13.
4. Luke 17:14.
5. Luke 17:14.
6. Luke 17:17–18.
7. Luke 17:19.

5 – The Power of Salvation
1. Luke 22:19.
2. Matthew 26:28.
3. Matthew 27:29–30.
4. Matthew 27:46.
5. John 19:32–34 & 36–37.
6. NAB Isaiah 53:4–5.
7. 1 Peter 2:24.

6 – The Power of Command
1. Luke 9:1–2.
2. Luke 9:6.
3. Luke 10:9.
4. Luke 10:17.
5. Luke 10:18–19.
6. Acts 9:34–35.
7. Mark 11:23.
8. Luke 4:39.
9. Acts 14:8.
10. Acts 14:9–10.
11. Acts 14:10.

7 – The Power of Prayer
1. Exodus 20:3–6.
2. Matthew 6:7–8.

8 – The Power of Forgiveness
1. 2 Corinthians 2:11.
2. Ephesians 4:26–27.
3. Matthew 6:9–13.
4. Matthew 6:10.
5. Matthew 6:12.
6. Matthew 6:14–15.

9 – The Power of God's Word
1. Matthew 21:22.
2. Matthew 18:19–20.
3. James 5:14–16.
4. Matthew 17:20.

10 – The Power of God's Calling
1. Luke 4:18–19.
2. Luke 4:21.
3. John 14:12.
4. Acts 6:8.
5. Acts 5:15.
6. Acts 19:11–12.
7. Mark 16:17–18.
8. Mark 16:15.

About the Author

Robert Abel's purpose and passion in life is speaking God's truth unto today's generation. He lives in Denver, Colorado, where he helps others heal through counseling sessions and healing seminars.

If you would like Robert to speak at your parish, or if you would like to share your healing testimony, please contact **www.HealingPowerMinistries.com**

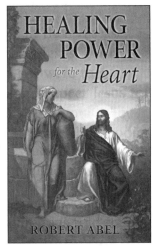

If you would like to participate in our healing ministry, please consider spreading the message of *The Healing Power of Jesus* to everybody you know who is sick or hurting. To purchase additional copies of this book for ministry purposes, or to make a donation, please use the following information:

Number of Copies	Ministry Price
5	$29
10	$49
20	$89

These prices include tax and free shipping within the United States. For shipments to other countries, please contact us. Thank you for your generous support.

Mail your payment to:

Valentine Publishing House
The Healing Power of Jesus
P.O. Box 27422
Denver, Colorado 80227